50 Sugar-Free Desserts for Healthier Indulgence

By: Kelly Johnson

Table of Contents

- Sugar-Free Chocolate Avocado Mousse
- Keto Cheesecake
- Chia Seed Pudding
- Coconut Flour Brownies
- Almond Flour Cookies
- Sugar-Free Banana Bread
- Dark Chocolate Bark with Nuts
- Sugar-Free Peanut Butter Cups
- Baked Cinnamon Apples
- Greek Yogurt Berry Parfait
- Sugar-Free Lemon Bars
- Keto Mug Cake
- Sugar-Free Matcha Ice Cream
- Flourless Chocolate Cake
- No-Bake Coconut Macaroons
- Sugar-Free Tiramisu
- Frozen Yogurt Bites
- Sugar-Free Carrot Cake
- Keto Pecan Pie
- Sugar-Free Chocolate Chip Cookies
- Raspberry Chia Jam Bars
- Sugar-Free Pumpkin Pie
- Sugar-Free Granola Bars
- Strawberry Coconut Popsicles
- Sugar-Free Fudge
- Chocolate-Covered Almonds
- Sugar-Free Peanut Butter Cookies
- Berry Almond Crumble
- Sugar-Free Mango Sorbet
- Sugar-Free Vanilla Pudding
- Low-Carb Lemon Cheesecake
- Sugar-Free Ice Cream Sandwiches
- Cacao Energy Balls
- Sugar-Free Hot Chocolate
- Avocado Brownies

- Sugar-Free Mocha Mousse
- Cinnamon Roasted Pecans
- Low-Carb Panna Cotta
- Sugar-Free Coconut Pudding
- Sugar-Free Snickerdoodles
- Almond Butter Blondies
- Keto Pumpkin Muffins
- Sugar-Free Chocolate-Covered Strawberries
- Blackberry Chia Pudding
- Coconut Flour Pancakes with Berries
- Low-Carb Zucchini Bread
- Sugar-Free Mocha Ice Cream
- Sugar-Free Protein Brownies
- Dark Chocolate Coconut Clusters
- Sugar-Free Chocolate Lava Cake

Sugar-Free Chocolate Avocado Mousse

Ingredients:

- 2 ripe avocados
- ¼ cup unsweetened cocoa powder
- ¼ cup sugar-free sweetener (erythritol or monk fruit)
- ½ cup unsweetened almond milk
- 1 tsp vanilla extract
- ¼ tsp salt
- Optional: Dark chocolate shavings or berries for garnish

Instructions:

1. **Blend Ingredients:** In a food processor, blend avocados, cocoa powder, sweetener, almond milk, vanilla, and salt until smooth.
2. **Chill & Serve:** Refrigerate for 30 minutes before serving. Garnish as desired.

Keto Cheesecake

Ingredients:

- **Crust:**
    - 1 cup almond flour
    - 2 tbsp butter, melted
    - 1 tbsp sugar-free sweetener
- **Filling:**
    - 16 oz cream cheese, softened
    - ½ cup sugar-free sweetener
    - 2 eggs
    - 1 tsp vanilla extract
    - ¼ cup heavy cream

Instructions:

1. **Prepare Crust:** Mix almond flour, butter, and sweetener. Press into a pan and bake at 350°F (175°C) for 10 minutes.
2. **Make Filling:** Beat cream cheese, sweetener, eggs, vanilla, and heavy cream until smooth.
3. **Bake & Chill:** Pour over crust and bake for 40 minutes. Cool and refrigerate before serving.

Chia Seed Pudding

Ingredients:

- ¼ cup chia seeds
- 1 cup unsweetened almond milk
- 1 tbsp sugar-free sweetener
- ½ tsp vanilla extract
- Optional: Berries or nuts for topping

Instructions:

1. **Mix Ingredients:** Stir chia seeds, almond milk, sweetener, and vanilla in a bowl.
2. **Refrigerate:** Chill for at least 2 hours (or overnight) until thick.
3. **Serve:** Stir well and top with berries or nuts.

Coconut Flour Brownies

Ingredients:

- ¼ cup coconut flour
- ¼ cup unsweetened cocoa powder
- ½ cup sugar-free sweetener
- 2 eggs
- ¼ cup melted butter or coconut oil
- ½ tsp vanilla extract
- ¼ tsp salt

Instructions:

1. **Mix Ingredients:** In a bowl, whisk eggs, butter, sweetener, cocoa powder, coconut flour, vanilla, and salt.
2. **Bake:** Pour batter into a greased pan and bake at 350°F (175°C) for 20-25 minutes.
3. **Cool & Serve:** Let cool before slicing.

Almond Flour Cookies

Ingredients:

- 1 cup almond flour
- ¼ cup sugar-free sweetener
- ¼ cup butter, melted
- 1 egg
- ½ tsp vanilla extract
- ¼ tsp baking soda
- ¼ cup sugar-free chocolate chips (optional)

Instructions:

1. **Make Dough:** Mix almond flour, sweetener, butter, egg, vanilla, and baking soda. Fold in chocolate chips.
2. **Bake:** Scoop dough onto a baking sheet and bake at 350°F (175°C) for 10-12 minutes.
3. **Cool & Serve:** Let cool before eating.

Sugar-Free Banana Bread

Ingredients:

- 2 ripe bananas, mashed
- 2 eggs
- 1 cup almond flour
- ¼ cup sugar-free sweetener
- ½ tsp cinnamon
- ½ tsp baking soda
- ¼ cup melted butter or coconut oil

Instructions:

1. **Make Batter:** Mix mashed bananas, eggs, almond flour, sweetener, cinnamon, baking soda, and butter.
2. **Bake:** Pour into a loaf pan and bake at 350°F (175°C) for 30-35 minutes.
3. **Cool & Serve:** Let cool before slicing.

Dark Chocolate Bark with Nuts

Ingredients:

- 1 cup sugar-free dark chocolate, melted
- ½ cup mixed nuts (almonds, walnuts, pecans)
- ¼ tsp sea salt

Instructions:

1. **Melt Chocolate:** Use a double boiler or microwave.
2. **Assemble:** Spread chocolate on parchment paper, sprinkle nuts and sea salt on top.
3. **Chill & Break:** Refrigerate until firm, then break into pieces.

Sugar-Free Peanut Butter Cups

Ingredients:

- 1 cup sugar-free dark chocolate, melted
- ½ cup natural peanut butter
- 1 tbsp sugar-free sweetener

Instructions:

1. **Make Peanut Butter Filling:** Mix peanut butter and sweetener.
2. **Layer in Molds:** Pour melted chocolate into molds, add peanut butter, then cover with more chocolate.
3. **Chill & Serve:** Refrigerate until firm.

Baked Cinnamon Apples

Ingredients:

- 2 apples, sliced
- 1 tbsp butter, melted
- 1 tsp cinnamon
- 1 tbsp sugar-free sweetener
- ½ tsp vanilla extract
- ¼ cup chopped nuts (optional)

Instructions:

1. **Preheat Oven:** Set to 375°F (190°C).
2. **Mix Ingredients:** Toss apple slices with butter, cinnamon, sweetener, and vanilla.
3. **Bake:** Spread on a baking dish and bake for 20 minutes.
4. **Serve:** Top with nuts or sugar-free whipped cream.

Greek Yogurt Berry Parfait

Ingredients:

- 1 cup Greek yogurt (unsweetened)
- ½ cup mixed berries (strawberries, blueberries, raspberries)
- 1 tbsp sugar-free sweetener
- ¼ cup chopped nuts or sugar-free granola

Instructions:

1. **Layer Ingredients:** In a glass, layer yogurt, sweetener, berries, and nuts.
2. **Repeat Layers:** Continue until the glass is full.
3. **Serve:** Enjoy immediately or chill for later.

Sugar-Free Lemon Bars

Ingredients:

- **Crust:**
    - 1 cup almond flour
    - 2 tbsp butter, melted
    - 1 tbsp sugar-free sweetener
- **Filling:**
    - ½ cup fresh lemon juice
    - 3 eggs
    - ¼ cup sugar-free sweetener
    - 1 tbsp coconut flour

Instructions:

1. **Preheat Oven:** Set to 350°F (175°C).
2. **Prepare Crust:** Mix almond flour, butter, and sweetener, press into a pan, and bake for 10 minutes.
3. **Make Filling:** Whisk eggs, lemon juice, sweetener, and coconut flour.
4. **Bake:** Pour over crust and bake for another 20 minutes.
5. **Cool & Serve:** Let cool before slicing.

Keto Mug Cake

Ingredients:

- 2 tbsp almond flour
- 1 tbsp cocoa powder
- 1 tbsp sugar-free sweetener
- ½ tsp baking powder
- 1 egg
- 1 tbsp melted butter
- 1 tbsp almond milk

Instructions:

1. **Mix Ingredients:** In a microwave-safe mug, whisk almond flour, cocoa powder, sweetener, baking powder, egg, butter, and almond milk.
2. **Microwave:** Cook for 60 seconds.
3. **Serve:** Let cool slightly before eating.

Sugar-Free Matcha Ice Cream

Ingredients:

- 1 cup heavy cream or coconut milk
- 2 tbsp sugar-free sweetener
- 1 tsp matcha powder
- ½ tsp vanilla extract

Instructions:

1. **Blend Ingredients:** Whisk together cream, sweetener, matcha, and vanilla.
2. **Freeze:** Pour into a container and freeze for at least 3 hours, stirring every 30 minutes.
3. **Serve:** Scoop and enjoy!

Flourless Chocolate Cake

Ingredients:

- ½ cup sugar-free dark chocolate, melted
- ¼ cup butter, melted
- 2 eggs
- ¼ cup cocoa powder
- 2 tbsp sugar-free sweetener

Instructions:

1. **Preheat Oven:** Set to 350°F (175°C).
2. **Mix Ingredients:** Whisk melted chocolate, butter, eggs, cocoa powder, and sweetener.
3. **Bake:** Pour into a greased pan and bake for 15-20 minutes.
4. **Cool & Serve:** Let cool before slicing.

No-Bake Coconut Macaroons

Ingredients:

- 1 cup shredded unsweetened coconut
- ¼ cup coconut oil
- 2 tbsp sugar-free sweetener
- ½ tsp vanilla extract

Instructions:

1. **Mix Ingredients:** Combine all ingredients in a bowl.
2. **Shape:** Scoop small portions and place on a lined baking sheet.
3. **Chill:** Refrigerate for at least 30 minutes before serving.

Sugar-Free Tiramisu

Ingredients:

- **Mascarpone Cream:**
    - 8 oz mascarpone cheese
    - ½ cup sugar-free sweetener
    - ½ cup heavy cream
    - 1 tsp vanilla extract
- **Layers:**
    - 1 cup strong coffee
    - ¼ cup sugar-free sweetener
    - 1 batch almond flour sponge cake or keto ladyfingers
    - 1 tbsp cocoa powder

Instructions:

1. **Make Coffee Mix:** Mix coffee and sweetener, then let cool.
2. **Make Cream:** Whisk mascarpone, heavy cream, sweetener, and vanilla until smooth.
3. **Assemble:** Layer soaked sponge cake with mascarpone cream in a dish.
4. **Chill & Serve:** Refrigerate for 2 hours, dust with cocoa powder before serving.

Frozen Yogurt Bites

Ingredients:

- 1 cup Greek yogurt
- ½ cup mixed berries
- 1 tbsp sugar-free sweetener

Instructions:

1. **Mix Ingredients:** Combine yogurt, sweetener, and berries.
2. **Spoon into Molds:** Drop spoonfuls onto a parchment-lined baking sheet.
3. **Freeze & Serve:** Freeze for 1 hour before enjoying.

Sugar-Free Carrot Cake

Ingredients:

- **Cake:**
    - 2 cups almond flour
    - 1 cup grated carrots
    - ½ cup sugar-free sweetener
    - ½ tsp baking soda
    - ½ tsp cinnamon
    - ½ tsp nutmeg
    - 3 eggs
    - ¼ cup melted coconut oil
    - 1 tsp vanilla extract
    - ½ cup chopped pecans (optional)
- **Frosting:**
    - 8 oz cream cheese, softened
    - 2 tbsp sugar-free sweetener
    - 1 tsp vanilla extract

Instructions:

1. **Preheat Oven:** Set to 350°F (175°C).
2. **Mix Wet & Dry Ingredients:** Whisk eggs, coconut oil, and vanilla. In a separate bowl, mix almond flour, sweetener, baking soda, cinnamon, and nutmeg.
3. **Combine:** Fold in grated carrots and pecans.
4. **Bake:** Pour into a greased pan and bake for 25-30 minutes.
5. **Frost & Serve:** Cool, then spread cream cheese frosting.

Keto Pecan Pie

Ingredients:

- **Crust:**
    - 1 ½ cups almond flour
    - 2 tbsp melted butter
    - 1 tbsp sugar-free sweetener
- **Filling:**
    - 1 cup pecans
    - ½ cup sugar-free sweetener
    - 2 eggs
    - ¼ cup butter, melted
    - 1 tsp vanilla extract

Instructions:

1. **Prepare Crust:** Mix almond flour, butter, and sweetener, press into a pie pan, and bake at 350°F (175°C) for 10 minutes.
2. **Make Filling:** Whisk eggs, sweetener, butter, and vanilla, then stir in pecans.
3. **Bake:** Pour filling over crust and bake for 30 minutes.

Sugar-Free Chocolate Chip Cookies

Ingredients:

- 1 cup almond flour
- ¼ cup sugar-free sweetener
- ¼ cup butter, melted
- 1 egg
- ½ tsp vanilla extract
- ¼ tsp baking soda
- ¼ cup sugar-free chocolate chips

Instructions:

1. **Preheat Oven:** Set to 350°F (175°C).
2. **Mix Ingredients:** Combine almond flour, sweetener, butter, egg, vanilla, and baking soda. Fold in chocolate chips.
3. **Bake:** Scoop onto a baking sheet and bake for 10-12 minutes.

Raspberry Chia Jam Bars

Ingredients:

- **Crust:**
    - 1 cup almond flour
    - ¼ cup butter, melted
    - 1 tbsp sugar-free sweetener
- **Filling:**
    - 1 cup raspberries
    - 2 tbsp chia seeds
    - 1 tbsp sugar-free sweetener

Instructions:

1. **Prepare Jam:** Cook raspberries, chia seeds, and sweetener until thick.
2. **Make Crust:** Mix almond flour, butter, and sweetener, press into a baking dish, and bake for 10 minutes.
3. **Assemble & Bake:** Spread jam over crust and bake for 10 more minutes.

Sugar-Free Pumpkin Pie

Ingredients:

- **Crust:**
    - 1 ½ cups almond flour
    - 2 tbsp melted butter
    - 1 tbsp sugar-free sweetener
- **Filling:**
    - 1 cup pumpkin puree
    - ½ cup heavy cream
    - ¼ cup sugar-free sweetener
    - 1 egg
    - 1 tsp pumpkin spice

Instructions:

1. **Prepare Crust:** Mix almond flour, butter, and sweetener, press into a pie pan, and bake at 350°F (175°C) for 10 minutes.
2. **Make Filling:** Whisk pumpkin, cream, sweetener, egg, and spice.
3. **Bake:** Pour into crust and bake for 40 minutes.

Sugar-Free Granola Bars

Ingredients:

- 1 cup almonds, chopped
- 1 cup sunflower seeds
- ½ cup shredded coconut
- ½ cup sugar-free sweetener
- ¼ cup almond butter
- ¼ cup coconut oil

Instructions:

1. **Melt Almond Butter & Oil:** Heat almond butter, coconut oil, and sweetener until combined.
2. **Mix Ingredients:** Stir in nuts, seeds, and coconut.
3. **Set & Chill:** Press into a pan and refrigerate until firm, then slice.

Strawberry Coconut Popsicles

Ingredients:

- 1 cup strawberries, blended
- 1 cup coconut milk
- 2 tbsp sugar-free sweetener
- 1 tsp vanilla extract

Instructions:

1. **Blend Ingredients:** Mix strawberries, coconut milk, sweetener, and vanilla.
2. **Freeze:** Pour into popsicle molds and freeze for 3-4 hours.

Sugar-Free Fudge

Ingredients:

- 1 cup sugar-free dark chocolate, melted
- ½ cup coconut oil
- ¼ cup sugar-free sweetener
- 1 tsp vanilla extract

Instructions:

1. **Melt Ingredients:** Mix melted chocolate, coconut oil, sweetener, and vanilla.
2. **Set & Chill:** Pour into a lined pan and refrigerate until firm.

Chocolate-Covered Almonds

Ingredients:

- 1 cup almonds
- 1 cup sugar-free dark chocolate, melted
- ¼ tsp sea salt

Instructions:

1. **Melt Chocolate:** Use a double boiler or microwave.
2. **Coat Almonds:** Toss almonds in melted chocolate, then spread on a baking sheet.
3. **Set & Serve:** Refrigerate until hardened, then sprinkle with sea salt.

Sugar-Free Peanut Butter Cookies

Ingredients:

- 1 cup natural peanut butter
- ½ cup sugar-free sweetener
- 1 egg
- ½ tsp vanilla extract
- ¼ tsp salt

Instructions:

1. **Preheat Oven:** Set to 350°F (175°C).
2. **Mix Ingredients:** Combine peanut butter, sweetener, egg, vanilla, and salt.
3. **Shape & Bake:** Roll into balls, press with a fork, and bake for 10 minutes.
4. **Cool & Serve:** Let cool before eating.

Berry Almond Crumble

Ingredients:

- **Filling:**
    - 2 cups mixed berries (strawberries, blueberries, raspberries)
    - 1 tbsp lemon juice
    - 2 tbsp sugar-free sweetener
- **Crumble Topping:**
    - ½ cup almond flour
    - ¼ cup chopped almonds
    - 2 tbsp melted butter
    - 1 tbsp sugar-free sweetener

Instructions:

1. **Preheat Oven:** Set to 350°F (175°C).
2. **Prepare Filling:** Mix berries, lemon juice, and sweetener in a baking dish.
3. **Make Crumble:** Combine almond flour, almonds, butter, and sweetener, then sprinkle over berries.
4. **Bake:** Cook for 20 minutes until golden.

Sugar-Free Mango Sorbet

Ingredients:

- 2 cups frozen mango chunks
- ½ cup unsweetened coconut milk
- 1 tbsp sugar-free sweetener
- 1 tsp lime juice

Instructions:

1. **Blend Ingredients:** Puree mango, coconut milk, sweetener, and lime juice until smooth.
2. **Freeze & Serve:** Freeze for 1 hour before serving.

Sugar-Free Vanilla Pudding

Ingredients:

- 2 cups unsweetened almond milk
- ¼ cup sugar-free sweetener
- 2 tbsp cornstarch
- 1 tsp vanilla extract
- 1 egg yolk

Instructions:

1. **Heat Milk:** Warm almond milk in a saucepan.
2. **Thicken Pudding:** Whisk in sweetener and cornstarch. Stir continuously until thickened.
3. **Add Vanilla & Egg:** Remove from heat, stir in vanilla and egg yolk.
4. **Chill & Serve:** Refrigerate before serving.

Low-Carb Lemon Cheesecake

Ingredients:

- **Crust:**
    - 1 cup almond flour
    - 2 tbsp melted butter
    - 1 tbsp sugar-free sweetener
- **Filling:**
    - 16 oz cream cheese, softened
    - ½ cup sugar-free sweetener
    - 2 eggs
    - ¼ cup lemon juice
    - 1 tsp vanilla extract

Instructions:

1. **Preheat Oven:** Set to 350°F (175°C).
2. **Prepare Crust:** Mix almond flour, butter, and sweetener, press into a pan, and bake for 10 minutes.
3. **Make Filling:** Beat cream cheese, sweetener, eggs, lemon juice, and vanilla until smooth.
4. **Bake:** Pour over crust and bake for 40 minutes.

Sugar-Free Ice Cream Sandwiches

Ingredients:

- **Cookies:**
    - 1 cup almond flour
    - ¼ cup sugar-free sweetener
    - ¼ cup butter, melted
    - 1 egg
    - ½ tsp vanilla extract
- **Ice Cream Filling:**
    - 1 cup sugar-free vanilla ice cream

Instructions:

1. **Make Cookies:** Mix almond flour, sweetener, butter, egg, and vanilla. Scoop onto a baking sheet and bake at 350°F (175°C) for 10 minutes.
2. **Assemble Sandwiches:** Let cookies cool, then sandwich ice cream between two cookies.
3. **Freeze:** Store in the freezer until firm.

Cacao Energy Balls

Ingredients:

- ½ cup almonds
- ½ cup walnuts
- 2 tbsp unsweetened cocoa powder
- ½ cup pitted dates or sugar-free sweetener
- 1 tbsp coconut oil
- 1 tsp vanilla extract

Instructions:

1. **Blend Ingredients:** Process almonds, walnuts, cocoa powder, dates/sweetener, coconut oil, and vanilla until sticky.
2. **Shape:** Roll into small balls.
3. **Chill & Serve:** Refrigerate before serving.

Sugar-Free Hot Chocolate

Ingredients:

- 1 cup unsweetened almond milk
- 2 tbsp unsweetened cocoa powder
- 1 tbsp sugar-free sweetener
- ½ tsp vanilla extract

Instructions:

1. **Heat Milk:** Warm almond milk in a saucepan.
2. **Whisk in Ingredients:** Stir in cocoa powder, sweetener, and vanilla.
3. **Serve:** Enjoy warm with sugar-free whipped cream.

Avocado Brownies

Ingredients:

- 1 ripe avocado, mashed
- ½ cup unsweetened cocoa powder
- ½ cup almond flour
- ¼ cup sugar-free sweetener
- 2 eggs
- ¼ cup melted coconut oil
- 1 tsp vanilla extract
- ½ tsp baking soda

Instructions:

1. **Preheat Oven:** Set to 350°F (175°C).
2. **Mix Ingredients:** Combine avocado, cocoa, almond flour, sweetener, eggs, coconut oil, vanilla, and baking soda.
3. **Bake:** Pour into a greased pan and bake for 20-25 minutes.

Sugar-Free Mocha Mousse

Ingredients:

- 1 cup heavy cream
- 2 tbsp unsweetened cocoa powder
- 1 tbsp sugar-free sweetener
- 1 tsp instant coffee
- ½ tsp vanilla extract

Instructions:

1. **Whip Cream:** Beat heavy cream, cocoa, sweetener, coffee, and vanilla until fluffy.
2. **Chill & Serve:** Refrigerate for 30 minutes before serving.

Cinnamon Roasted Pecans

Ingredients:

- 2 cups pecans
- 1 egg white
- 1 tbsp water
- ½ cup sugar-free sweetener
- 1 tsp cinnamon
- ½ tsp salt

Instructions:

1. **Preheat Oven:** Set to 300°F (150°C).
2. **Coat Pecans:** Whisk egg white and water until frothy, toss with pecans.
3. **Add Seasoning:** Mix in sweetener, cinnamon, and salt.
4. **Bake:** Spread on a baking sheet and bake for 30 minutes, stirring halfway.

Low-Carb Panna Cotta

Ingredients:

- 1 cup heavy cream
- ½ cup unsweetened almond milk
- ¼ cup sugar-free sweetener
- 1 tsp vanilla extract
- 1 tsp gelatin
- 2 tbsp water

Instructions:

1. **Dissolve Gelatin:** Sprinkle gelatin over water and let sit for 5 minutes.
2. **Heat Cream & Sweetener:** Warm heavy cream, almond milk, and sweetener in a saucepan (do not boil).
3. **Mix Gelatin & Chill:** Stir in gelatin and vanilla. Pour into molds and refrigerate for 4 hours.

Sugar-Free Coconut Pudding

Ingredients:

- 1 can (13.5 oz) unsweetened coconut milk
- ¼ cup sugar-free sweetener
- 1 tsp vanilla extract
- 1 tbsp cornstarch or gelatin

Instructions:

1. **Heat Coconut Milk:** Warm coconut milk and sweetener in a saucepan.
2. **Thicken:** Whisk in cornstarch/gelatin until smooth.
3. **Chill & Serve:** Pour into cups and refrigerate until set.

Sugar-Free Snickerdoodles

Ingredients:

- 1 cup almond flour
- ¼ cup sugar-free sweetener
- ¼ cup butter, melted
- 1 egg
- ½ tsp vanilla extract
- ½ tsp baking soda
- 1 tsp cinnamon

Instructions:

1. **Preheat Oven:** Set to 350°F (175°C).
2. **Mix Dough:** Combine all ingredients until a soft dough forms.
3. **Shape & Coat:** Roll into balls, coat with extra cinnamon and sweetener.
4. **Bake:** Place on a baking sheet and bake for 10-12 minutes.

Almond Butter Blondies

Ingredients:

- 1 cup almond butter
- ½ cup sugar-free sweetener
- 2 eggs
- ½ tsp baking soda
- 1 tsp vanilla extract
- ¼ cup sugar-free chocolate chips (optional)

Instructions:

1. **Preheat Oven:** Set to 350°F (175°C).
2. **Mix Ingredients:** Stir together almond butter, sweetener, eggs, baking soda, and vanilla.
3. **Bake:** Pour into a greased pan and bake for 20 minutes.
4. **Cool & Serve:** Let cool before slicing.

Keto Pumpkin Muffins

Ingredients:

- 1 cup almond flour
- ½ cup pumpkin puree
- ¼ cup sugar-free sweetener
- 2 eggs
- ½ tsp baking soda
- 1 tsp cinnamon
- ½ tsp nutmeg
- ¼ cup melted butter

Instructions:

1. **Preheat Oven:** Set to 350°F (175°C).
2. **Mix Ingredients:** Whisk together all ingredients until smooth.
3. **Bake:** Pour into muffin tins and bake for 20-25 minutes.

Sugar-Free Chocolate-Covered Strawberries

Ingredients:

- 10 fresh strawberries
- ½ cup sugar-free dark chocolate, melted

Instructions:

1. **Melt Chocolate:** Use a microwave or double boiler.
2. **Dip Strawberries:** Coat each strawberry in melted chocolate.
3. **Chill & Serve:** Refrigerate until the chocolate hardens.

Blackberry Chia Pudding

Ingredients:

- ¼ cup chia seeds
- 1 cup unsweetened almond milk
- ½ cup blackberries (fresh or frozen)
- 1 tbsp sugar-free sweetener
- ½ tsp vanilla extract

Instructions:

1. **Blend Blackberries:** Mash or blend blackberries with sweetener and vanilla.
2. **Mix Chia & Milk:** Stir chia seeds into the almond milk, then mix in the blackberry puree.
3. **Refrigerate:** Chill for at least 2 hours (or overnight) until thick.
4. **Serve:** Stir well and top with extra blackberries.

Coconut Flour Pancakes with Berries

Ingredients:

- ¼ cup coconut flour
- 2 eggs
- ¼ cup unsweetened almond milk
- 1 tbsp sugar-free sweetener
- ½ tsp baking powder
- ½ tsp vanilla extract
- ¼ cup mixed berries

Instructions:

1. **Make Batter:** Whisk eggs, almond milk, sweetener, baking powder, and vanilla. Stir in coconut flour.
2. **Cook Pancakes:** Heat a nonstick pan, pour small rounds, and cook for 2 minutes per side.
3. **Serve:** Top with fresh berries and sugar-free syrup.

Low-Carb Zucchini Bread

Ingredients:

- 2 cups almond flour
- 1 cup grated zucchini
- ½ cup sugar-free sweetener
- 3 eggs
- ¼ cup melted butter
- ½ tsp baking soda
- 1 tsp cinnamon
- ½ tsp vanilla extract

Instructions:

1. **Preheat Oven:** Set to 350°F (175°C).
2. **Mix Ingredients:** Stir together almond flour, zucchini, sweetener, eggs, butter, baking soda, cinnamon, and vanilla.
3. **Bake:** Pour into a greased loaf pan and bake for 40 minutes.
4. **Cool & Serve:** Let cool before slicing.

Sugar-Free Mocha Ice Cream

Ingredients:

- 1 cup heavy cream or coconut milk
- ¼ cup sugar-free sweetener
- 1 tbsp unsweetened cocoa powder
- 1 tsp instant coffee
- ½ tsp vanilla extract

Instructions:

1. **Blend Ingredients:** Mix all ingredients until smooth.
2. **Freeze:** Pour into a container and freeze for 3 hours, stirring every 30 minutes.
3. **Serve:** Scoop and enjoy!

Sugar-Free Protein Brownies

Ingredients:

- ½ cup almond flour
- ¼ cup chocolate protein powder
- ¼ cup unsweetened cocoa powder
- ½ cup sugar-free sweetener
- 2 eggs
- ¼ cup melted butter
- ½ tsp vanilla extract
- ½ tsp baking powder

Instructions:

1. **Preheat Oven:** Set to 350°F (175°C).
2. **Mix Ingredients:** Combine almond flour, protein powder, cocoa, sweetener, eggs, butter, vanilla, and baking powder.
3. **Bake:** Pour into a greased pan and bake for 20 minutes.
4. **Cool & Serve:** Let cool before slicing.

Dark Chocolate Coconut Clusters

Ingredients:

- 1 cup unsweetened shredded coconut
- ½ cup sugar-free dark chocolate, melted
- ¼ cup chopped nuts (optional)

Instructions:

1. **Melt Chocolate:** Use a microwave or double boiler.
2. **Mix Ingredients:** Stir shredded coconut and nuts into melted chocolate.
3. **Set & Chill:** Drop spoonfuls onto a lined baking sheet and refrigerate until firm.

Sugar-Free Chocolate Lava Cake

Ingredients:

- ½ cup sugar-free dark chocolate, melted
- ¼ cup almond flour
- 2 tbsp sugar-free sweetener
- 2 eggs
- ¼ cup butter, melted
- ½ tsp vanilla extract

Instructions:

1. **Preheat Oven:** Set to 375°F (190°C).
2. **Mix Ingredients:** Whisk eggs, melted chocolate, butter, sweetener, vanilla, and almond flour.
3. **Bake:** Pour into greased ramekins and bake for 10-12 minutes until edges are firm but the center is soft.
4. **Serve:** Enjoy warm with sugar-free whipped cream.

www.ingramcontent.com/pod-product-compliance
Lightning Source LLC
LaVergne TN
LVHW081504060526
838201LV00056BA/2926